Dear Family,

What's the best way to help your child love reading?

Find good books like this one to share—and read together!

Here are some tips.

●**Take a "picture walk."** Look at all the pictures before you read. Talk about what you see.

●**Take turns.** Read to your child. Ham it up! Use different voices for different characters, and read with feeling! Then listen as your child reads to you, or explains the story in his or her own words.

●**Point out words as you read.** Help your child notice how letters and sounds go together. Point out unusual or difficult words that your child might not know. Talk about those words and what they mean.

●**Ask questions.** Stop to ask questions as you read. For example: "What do you think will happen next?" "How would you feel if that happened to you?"

●**Read every day.** Good stories are worth reading more than once! Read signs, labels, and even cereal boxes with your child. Visit the library to take out more books. And look for other JUST FOR YOU! BOOKS you and your child can share!

The Editors

To "OKC Kid Writers," an awesome critique group;
my husband Edmond, who is my foundation;
and to my amazing children, Leslie, Eddy, and Allison.
—GH

To my sister Pede—whose
limitless talent and creativity amaze us all!
—SW

Library of Congress Cataloging-in-Publication Data

Hooks, Gwendolyn.
    Three's a crowd / by Gwendolyn Hooks ; illustrated by Sylvia Walker.
        p. cm.—(Just for you! Level 3)
    Summary: Keisha is very unhappy when Val spoils their Saturday fun by bringing along Mya, a new girl in her neighborhood, but soon realizes that three is not such a bad number after all. Includes activity ideas for parents and children.
    ISBN 0-439-56865-X (pbk.)
    [1. Jealousy—Fiction. 2. Best friends—Fiction. 3. Friendship—Fiction. 4. African Americans—Fiction.] I. Title: Three is a crowd. II. Walker, Sylvia, ill. III. Title. IV. Series.
    PZ7.H76635Th 2004
    [E]—dc22   2004042913

17 16 15 14 13 12 11   10 11 12 13 14/0
            Printed in the U.S.A. 40 • First Scholastic Printing, February 2004

Three's a Crowd

by Gwendolyn Hooks
Illustrated by Sylvia Walker

JUST FOR YOU!™
Level 3

It was Saturday. Keisha always met Val in the park on Saturdays. They rode their bikes and had adventures together—just the two of them.

This Saturday, Keisha got a big surprise. Val had brought another girl along! "Hey, Keisha. This is Mya," said Val. "Her family just moved to my street."

Keisha's heart sank. She did not want a new girl riding with them. Three was not a fun number. It was an odd number. There was always one left over.

Mya smiled, but Keisha turned and walked to the pond. "The ducks look hungry," Keisha told Val. "Did you bring bread?"

"Sure. I have enough for all of us," said Val.

"The ducks won't take bread crumbs from you," Keisha said to Mya. "They don't know you."

"Here, try it, Mya," said Val.

Mya tossed bread into the water.
QUACK! QUACK! QUACK!
The ducks flapped their wings.
They paddled to Mya, ate her
crumbs, and quacked for more.

Mya laughed. She tossed more crumbs into the water.

Keisha stuffed her bread into her pocket. She did not want to feed the ducks any more.

"Let's go to Miss Pat's," Keisha said. She jumped on her bike.

Val and Mya got on theirs, too.

"Miss Pat bakes the best cinnamon rolls," Val told Mya. "She lets us be her taste testers."

"But she can spare only two rolls," said Keisha.

"We can share," said Val.

Keisha was the first one to reach Miss Pat's cart. "Mmmmm!" Keisha smelled cinnamon. She saw the warm icing melting onto the fresh baked rolls. She could not wait to bite into one!

"Look!" said Val. Three rolls sat on a plate.

"I see I have a new tester," said Miss Pat.

Val and Mya soon had icing on their cheeks and chins. Keisha was not hungry any more.

"What's next?" asked Mya.

"We'll show you our secret place," said Val.

Keisha couldn't believe it! They had promised not to tell anyone about the secret place. Well, maybe they had not exactly promised, but Val knew it was their special place.

Why did Val have to bring Mya? Saturday was for best friends—just the two of them. They had matching necklaces to show it.

Mya didn't have one. Mya didn't need one!

"Let's go!" said Val.
Keisha pedaled fast.

Suddenly Mya yelled, "Watch out!"
Keisha ducked and missed the tree branch.

"You're lucky Mya is with us," said Val.

Keisha did not feel lucky.

It didn't take long to get to the secret place. "Look!" Val told Mya. "It's the back of the zoo."

"The lions are extra hungry in the mornings," Keisha said. "They'll look over here. Then we'll jump on our bikes and ride!"

Who would ride away first?
Keisha was sure it would be Mya.

"They're just lying in the sun,"
Mya said.

"Sh-h-h-h!" said Keisha and Val
at the same time.

A lion raised his head.

The lion looked at the girls.
"Come on!" Val yelled.
Both Val and Mya ran, but
Keisha did not move.
She was not afraid of a lion.

R O A R!

Now Keisha ran! She tripped on
a rock and fell with a thud. Her
arms and legs wouldn't move. She
could almost feel the lion's breath
burning her neck. Her life was over.

"Keisha! Get up!" said Mya.

"We can't lift you," Val said.

"Go!" Keisha cried out. "Don't try to save me. He'll eat you, too!"

"Keisha, he's just yawning," said Mya.

Keisha lifted her head.

Mya was right. She was safe. They had come back for her. Maybe she was wrong about the number three.

"Come on," said Val. "You look silly lying on the ground."

Keisha felt silly. She got up. Laughing, she brushed the dirt off of her clothes. Val and Mya laughed, too.

"Are you riding with us next Saturday?" Val asked Mya.

Mya looked at Keisha.

"Of course she is," said Keisha. "We'll have another adventure— just the three of us!"

Here are some fun things for you to do.

What Do YOU Say?

The title of this story comes from an old saying: "Two's company and three's a crowd."

How do YOU know that Keisha thinks this saying is true? Do you think Val and Mya believe it? Why?

How do YOU know that Keisha has changed her mind by the time the story ends?

Think about you and your friends. Do YOU think the saying is true? Tell why or why not.

Give an example based on something that happened to YOU in real life.

YOUR Message

The "best friends" necklace that Keisha and Val wear sends a message to everyone who sees them.

Think about designing a necklace or T-shirt that says something important about YOU. What would it say?

Draw a picture to show what YOUR necklacc or T-shirt would look like. Write a sentence or two about what this message means to you.

▲▲▲▲TOGETHER TIME ▲▲▲▲

Make some time to share ideas about the story with your young reader! Here are some activities you can try. There are no right or wrong answers!

Think About It: Keisha was not happy when Val showed up with Mya! Ask your child, "Can you think of something that Val could have done to make meeting Mya easier for Keisha? How do you think Mya felt about meeting Keisha?"

Talk About It: The park the girls go to is great! If you and your child could go there, which place would you most like to visit? Look for a park near your home. You might plan to take a trip there, and have an adventure together.

Act It Out: Invite your child to play the part of one of the girls in the story. Ask your child to tell about the day in the park. What would this character say was the best thing that happened? What was the worst thing?

Meet the Author

GWENDOLYN HOOKS says, "When I was a child, my father was in the Air Force and we lived on the base. On Saturday mornings, I rode my bike around my neighborhood and pretended I was having adventures. After I grew up, I went on adventures with my children. We even found a place at the zoo where we could peek at the hyenas, just as Keisha and her friends peek at the lions."

Gwen Hooks taught math before becoming a stay-at-home mom. About ten years ago, she began writing stories. Now Gwen also runs writing workshops for children and educators. She and her family live in Oklahoma City, Oklahoma. Her other book in the JUST FOR YOU! series is *The Mystery of the Missing Dog.*

Meet the Artist

SYLVIA WALKER says, "When I was in elementary school, a new girl moved to our town and was assigned to my class. Our teacher asked me to show her around. We became best friends immediately, and we still keep in touch with each other today. Best friends are forever!"

Sylvia is a native of Pasadena, California, and now lives in Philadelphia, Pennsylvania. She studied at the California Institute of Arts in Los Angeles and earned a Bachelor of Fine Arts degree. Sylvia uses watercolor, pencil, ink, and acrylic to create her artwork. Her works include paintings on canvas, children's fashion illustration, as well as many children's books. She has illustrated another book in the JUST FOR YOU! series, *What Do You Know? Snow!*